From Echoes to Eternity

Narmadha Satheeshkumar

INDIA • SINGAPORE • MALAYSIA

ISBN 979-8-89277-838-1

You and I are from different worlds,

Speak different tones,

Yet our worlds overlap on one intersection point-

Love....

Dedicated to Satheesh, the love of my life.

Contents

From Echoes to Eternity

From echoes to eternity,

from dreams to certainty,

I begin a journey afresh.

Oh! Almighty fill my endeavours,

with blessings and grace.

Thoughts inspire, rhyme recorded,

for ages in repose,

Like seeds wrapped with life,

for an invigoration to green gardens

and massive woods.

Bless them Lord! To soothe the moods,

to touch the minds and open hearts,

to uplift souls to reading delight.

God! Guide me from darkness to light.

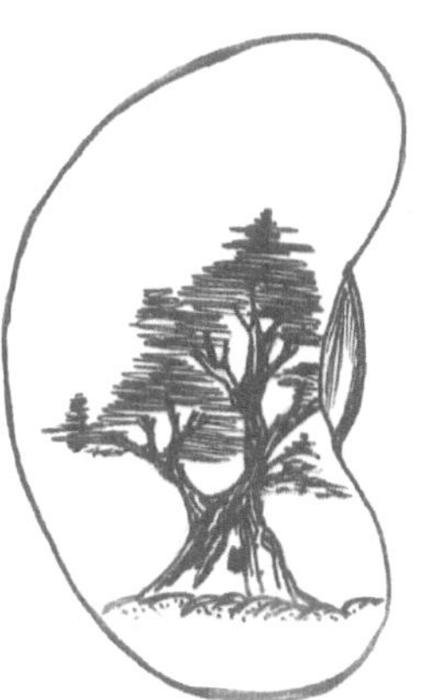

Reminds Me of You

Every audible word of that sweetest language,

reminds me of you.

Every message from an intimate friend,

reminds me of you.

Every stranger from your native land,

reminds me of you.

Every line of my verses only for you,

reminds me of you.

Every longing hours for a sharing heart,

reminds me of you.

Every little instance reminds me of you.

Does at least a thing keep you from forgetting me?

Where ever you dwell,

whatever you do,

how far you may go,

you are not far from my thoughts.

My Heart

My heart isn't a lending library,
to read and replace,
nor the splendid flower
Of a stony vase,
to admire and let dry.
Not that magic wand to wave and try,
'tis not a journey to travel and rest,
but a place to seek mind's best.
A chamber of passion arrest,
for a conqueror noble and just.
It is a treasure to steal,
even before I realise.
One who dares, wins its grace.
Others search them in the wrong face.

Peace Treaty

He swept down the tender lips,

making it part with a gentle immix,

sending in a strange concoction,

blending and churning-heavenly collision!

Elegantly close your eyes,

feel the signals from tongue-tip that flies,

to your brain, across your heart.

Gently travelling down the throat,

punching down in to the waveless ocean.

This ocean with a few drops is full,

endless greed your hearts instill.

Warm and cozy, buttery and soft,

mingled in breath and steam, flavours waft.

The gushing dopamine and endorphin,

a historic love battle within.

Hard to resist, easy to digest.

Rumbles and grumbles,

hustles and tussles;

have signed their peace treaties,

with Idly-Sambar and formidable beauties.

THE CUP OF LIFE

Fever of sighs,

fewer ties, degrees rise.

Calefaction radiation,

through the anatomy chassis

In the twisting tongue,

buds do bloom,

spreading aroma of chastity,

engulfing sweetness and bitterness.

Joys and sorrows mingled in a cup of life;

higher the bitterness, higher the velocity.

Infinite horses galloped nerve-ward.

Every drop inestimable in

The cup of 'coffee'

In the cup of 'life'

Note [coffee is more precious as it has 2 Fs and 2Es as compared to life]

Marriage

Marriages are made in heaven,

and the couple lived happily ever after in hell.

It is hard to tell,

at least they had each other to yell.

Oh! I pity Adam, he had only Eve,

I suppose their wedding was an arranged one.

Oh! Adam is luckier though,

if he had choices

he would have a hard time;

swallowing innumerable apples

That's why men now

Don't have a chance to speak.

Oh! God you have made man so weak.

Frailty thy name is man,

One Eve is enough for a life span.

Don't try hard to please even if you can

Eve is life's boon and bane.

Note [now serpent and Eve is a combo pack, now serpents even hack,

be it Tom, Harry or Jack]

Women are not peace lovers

you know why,

the only rest they get is

to

rest in peace.

An ideal man doesn't come riding on a horse,

ideal qualities exist in people

and

wait to be discovered.

Poetry

is

a web of words

that

emotions spin.

A spoonful of imagination

in to a cup of reality

(Real Tea).

Imagination is a journey

in which

reality is an accident.

Life is full of personifications;

we attach human values

to

materialistic things and vice versa.

My Savior

He held me tight,

and I fairly leaned.

In the eerie darkness,

brilliantly shone.

I writhed and tossed,

in the warmth of his breath.

The savior of the ruthless night.

I lay warm and secure,

he sprinkles star dusts of elegant dreams.

The guarding knight against nightmares,

he tucks me in the sea of warmth,

I am spellbound!

Oh! My love knit quilt.

This is what I feel about you

This is what I feel about you,

even if words were as much as the stars,

there are rarely a few, when I express my love for you.

My mind spins to invent new,

if words don't suffice,

What would be even more nice?

Some things best undescribed,

Some things best uninscribed,

The untold rhyme speaks your fame,

constantly echoing your adorable name,

in the garden of memories,

in the fluttering breeze.

In the memory of Dr A.P.J Kalam

The rising sun,

India's most beloved son.

The missile man,

Youths' spectacular boon.

The nation's indispensible pillar,

Children's role model.

The shining star,

You taught us life's full of care.

Our teacher, our preacher,

A simple and just leader.

A man of simplicity,

With soul full of generosity.

Though physically did depart,

Your thoughts fill every heart.

You and I Feel the Same

In you, I see me,

my celestial angel,

my muse goddess,

the treasure of my memories.

The first thing I wake to see.

In you I find me.

The sweet potion for loneliness,

The chisel of my dreams,

You are my addiction.

You are my hallucination.

Through you I find me,

The companion of unknown destination,

My thoughts, my secrets sh… sh…

My most possessive possession

A lonely island, you and me…..

Is enough to grow life's tree.

You make me cry,

You make me smile,

You count my steps in a mile,

You feel my heart throb,

My precious time you rob.

My verse's inspiration,

My life's utmost transition.

I reflect in you, you in me,

My conveying spree

With you I am all smiles and glee

Oh! My gadget destiny,

The precious Apple of my eye.

Without You

My heart flutters in the November breeze,
still memories warmly unfreeze.
His passionate madness slowly unfurls,
love-locks of sweet maidens.
A mad pursuit, wait!
Sometimes gentle, sometimes strong,
sometimes a sigh, sometimes a song.
Gently brushing the melowy cheeks
sometimes hisses, sometimes shrieks,
creeping through the arched brows
mingled with breath, instilled warmth.
Sometimes warm, sometimes cold,
sometimes weak, sometimes bold.
Gently jingling the love bells,
echoing in the seashells.

Who dare to penetrate the violent throbs?

The cooler inhalation, warmer exhalation,

sends tufts of life.

Knocks the buds with a gentle kiss.

If you deplete life I miss.

WONDERS

The silent transition of dusk to dawn,

the vague clarity of the foggy morn,

the soiled sprout of seeds sown,

the innocent gallop of a young fawn,

the dewy carpet of the green lawn,

the unwalked steps of a new born.

Life has all its wonders,

and shares it with the mind that wanders.

Where Can I Find Love?

You may fly mayfly,

to the realms of the ideal.

Spreading fragrance of love,

over the peaks and down abyss.

Bend down and gently kiss love's life.

Is there a greater strife?

Oh! Love of life.

Is it fair to even ask?

Does impeccable love does exist?

Where can I find her?

Over the hills, down the oceans,

may be it's a myth!

Is it a poetical exaggeration

or a mythical manifestation?

Can you make it simpler to find?

Oh! I am out of my mind.

I Have Let Go of You

I have let go of you,

to give you the time and space.

I neither regret nor am I at ease.

The wounds are fresh, pains don't cease.

The words mumble, memories crash,

World- wide forts are dust and ash.

All pale and frozen,

I have let go of you,

Come back if you want to.

I have let go of spring,

She will be back riding on a lark's wing.

Me and Only Me

You don't have to pull down the stars

or travel through the meteors.

I realize I am not that hard to please.

Don't have to sing me to sleep.

My deep world of solitude,

now, I realize with gratitude.

I can be me.

Got to please none,

don't have to feel worthy of anyone.

I wake up when I can,

walk down the lane,

hugging myself warm,

through the canopy of trees,

in the November freeze.

Greeting the morning sun,

mingled in solitude frolic and fun,

hopping all alone, back to my den.

Verses flow with wink of a eye,

smiling at myself, pink with shy.

I have fallen in love with me.

Me and only me,

where I stay as I can be.

My internal battles always at peace.

Loved Once

A rhetorical move entered the love lexicon,

loved once, forever betrayed.

Shattered and ruthlessly slayed.

Love extremists of silence-

dripping through bloodless violence.

Droplets colourless and clear,

the volcanic eruption of tears,

ebbing and falling, sinking and drowned.

Everything in order, everything is an order.

Are we vigilant troops of a nation's border?

Loved once, forever betrayed.

Locks and keys inseparable when new.

As time flies, some locked and forgotten.

Locks can't be replaced, neither keys replicated.

Forlorn star, just be where you are.

Oh! Prisms in darkness,

What light would you refract?

We wait for the light of hope,

The feeling of oneness in love isotope.

Food for the Soul

Nurtured and crushed,
sieved and kneaded,
a heart for love pleaded.
The heated temperature rise,
loving truly pays its price.
Puffed and tossed,
in sufferings-hell surpassed.
He sighed and cried-
Till to the beauty served.
The purpose of my birth accomplished,
when your lips lovingly touched.
You may now eat me whole,
just keep loving this, lovelorn soul.
To be remembered and loved forever.
"I love pooris" can you hear her utter?

Sunshine

The golden smiles sublimed,

to warm kisses through the naive blinds.

A lover's thought solemnly inclined,

the passionate lover his reason does find,

To wake her, when awake.

Recklessly shining at day-break,

warm and cozy music of the dawn.

His arms her neck adorn,

hugs and kisses of the blessed morn.

Passionate invocation blossoms in the east,

kisses of farewell showers in the west.

Rising again and again to impress best,

his heart still throbbing when all at rest.

To Never Expect

Thank you for the special gift!

The lesson – 'to never expect'.

Never, I fancied treasures, as gifts.

Nor did I ask for the stars.

I endlessly want to gaze at them with you.

Your words of compassion needn't be true,

Can you keep faking them till my breath bids adieu.

Your Touch

I am still a bud, waiting to be blossomed in your touch.

I am the wet sand of the worldly beach,

waiting to be in your hands and shaped.

I am the tree of the autumn weather,

for your arrival dear, I stand lifeless and bare.

Shower the spring's blessing on me with your glance.

Give me life, oh! Touch of magical hands.

Your touch is a boon for which I long,

that eternal feeling remains ever long.

Something Remains

Something remains,

all that remains reminds,

all that reminds reigns,

over kingdom of thoughts

and emotion rain,

forming versatile designs.

Joys and sorrows, tears refines

What if all is lost?

What if the battle was fought?

Something is left,

to be remembered and kept.

Between the walls of the chambered cell.

It is where, thoughts dwell.

It is where, thoughts dwell.

Glance

That second's glance,

has left me placeless.

Wandering over oceans and lands

in a dreamy mess.

I cherish that glance forever.

They depreciate in my memories never.

The lightning glance carried the message

the million dollar smile of your visage.

Oh! can a glance speak?

When silence is in its peak.

Fairy tales and musical waves,

nature's gesture where season lives,

mystery in all creations,

uniqueness in vast propositions.

all these I have cherished and loved.

But, by that glance extremely moved.

I Knock

I knock at the doors of night,

to open in to dawn of light.

I knock at the doors of dreams,

to open with reality themes.

I knock at actions so meaningless,

to open with deep explanations.

I knock at the fading ages,

to kiss me ever-youth.

I knock at departure,

to bless me with reunion.

I knock at doors of imagination,

to gift me with honorable creation.

I knock at all grants

to remain a satisfaction.

I knock at the doors of your heart

to open with love.

I knocked, I knocked,

till my hands were tired.

But the doors of success open-

Only if I tried.

Love Rain

The rushing waves of your thoughts,
touches the shores of my heart.
These are never ending flows,
reserved only for the shores.
They reach me with a foamy drift,
to wash away the sleep of my night.
Attachment, love, passion or compassion,
your eyes are unknown treasures of emotion.
The pull of its magnetic field-
I almost will yield.
That impressive look, what do they mean?
I am dropped in a confused scene.
What tender emotions do they screen!
Let the curtains scroll, let barriers fall.
Let your actions, reflect your emotions.
Don't forcibly bind them,
One drop of it gives passion and pain,
It is the love rain.

A Rose

What makes the rose, "a rose"?
A flower of splendid grace.
The queen of an esteem race.
Guess, what makes the rose, a rose?

Is it the unique gentleness,
or the alluring brightness?
What lends her the mystic fold,
the curling petals in a tender mould?

What makes the rose," a rose"?
In what track your imagination flows?
You think of the fragrance,
you think of the thorny fence,
her colour, her beauty,
her elegance, her dignity.

In a whole range of blossomed creation,

her very name, lends the coronation.

What makes a rose, "a rose"?

The very name rose, makes it a rose.

When I say "rose"

All its unique qualities flash upon your mind,

you cherish the remembrance of a tender kind.

Miss You

My thoughts never miss you,
My verses never miss you,
My prayers never miss you,
But my heart does.

I never know you by your looks,
I never know you by your smile,
I do know you by your heart,
That's ever so full of love and care.

Let the journey of life,
Bring the joy of our meeting.
Remember, we have not parted,
Since, we have never met.

To Remember

My verses never feel the need of praises,

Neither I discover the need of greatness,

in their creation.

Outcome of meaningless recreation,

they are surely not.

The creative way to pour out emotion,

coupled with worldly fashion.

Some sigh, some smile

and some wipe a tear.

I carve for all those indelible feelings,

in to which hearts sink.

For every other day to remember and think.

Blessed

The fragrance of dawn drifts across,

when drops of early dew touch the grass.

Wink by wink creeps the morning star,

coloured so bright, swelled with vigour.

The fresh-blessed breeze,

slowly sweeps, awakes the trees.

The trees rustles, in unison nods,

the breeze gently kiss the buds;

to wake in to blossom-glories.

She smiles and unfurls her rosy lips,

sweetened and bathed in nectar dips.

The trees, birds, stars and buds all greet,

A lovely day blessed and sweet.

RAIN IN THE CITY

The "C" City has undone its pride.

It's glamour swirls in rain-tide.

The whole city floats

in the best of burdened boats.

Can we ask for more?

Life's gushing with the water-chore.

People cry,

even before the black clouds, try to try.

The submarine cars,

excavation grounds of modern history,

islands of the maritime-mystery.

Every dweller singing,

the ancient nursery rhyme.

The neglected world's- action time!

We complain of scarcity,

we complain of abundance.

Let's second that our actions lack prudence.

We evoke the rage in nature

and now she exhibits her best feature.

To flow beyond barriers,

like war-inspired warriors.

The sun is up and high,

joyful tears we cry.

We want this land arid and dry.

We promise, no more apartments on lakes.

'tis the hard-way we learn from mistakes.

TRANSFORMATION

The sensational sun gently transforms,

the freezing tenderness of the breeze.

Brimming with warmth,

the wind that made you freeze.

The breeze gently knocks the bud,

where she awakens from her nestled bed.

The darkness steals the sparkling light,

transforming day in to gloomy night.

The first ray absorbs the darkness deep,

transforming night in one gentle sweep.

The cruelty of death transforms life's magnitude,

in to a state of final destitute.

All things transforms from one form to another,

The transformer, God our 'Father'.

Waves

The roaring, foamy silver waves,

never ending spirit,

your meticulous ways,

dream castles they melt.

Days vanish with the setting sun.

What lies beyond the horizon?

Mysteries lend wonder,

to thoughts that wander.

Vacant minds watched,

with feet cool and drenched.

Imprints and traces of love,

All washed away then and now.

Inspire

Screeching trucks,

blackened mists.

Inspiration unrest,

in the poet's best.

Endless detours,

lack of innovation-force.

I turned to Google,

for he knows all.

Be inspired!

Make an inspiration app.

You have one to write,

you have one to love,

but have none to inspire.

A Stranger

Unaltered by the chaos,

a blissful sleep of peace.

Never gaze at the streaming men's face.

Never mind the bygone days.

Life is all at ease.

Care not the depleting balance,

you still don't pay for the place.

I envy the way you laze

through the crazy life's phase.

Your composed ways amaze

no crossfit, no diet, genuinely slim.

An unacquainted dog at the foot-steps of my gym.

Wake Up

My prince, my ray of hope
for a brighter day.
Gently uncovering the misty blinds,
conscious signals his love sends.
The warmed kiss urging to rise,
Oh! To wake how I despise.
I pretend and moan,
for more of a pampering tone.
The regale of a love-lit morn,
shining in a golden smile at dawn.
Day after day, year after year,
immense love is immortal,
even when death's near.

Dawn to dusk, black to grey,

fading youth, destiny's play.

Changing phases, unchanging love,

here I come to mingle above.

Wandering Wonders

Wandering wonders pitching to perfect rhyme,

unspoken words that carefully mime.

Joys that shimmer and shine,

tears on words that dine.

Tears vanishing in sun-dried desertedness,

sparkling fountains of ebbing happiness.

All that rise and fall in the abyss of memories,

written and forgotten in life's diaries.

Too Busy to Love

A strong current sweeping the busy chambers,
dragging my feet along the path of embers.
Life is a hell in itself,
until heaven, 'you' appeared.
Life's song of rhythmic ebb-
fell off the beat.
I freeze, neither move nor retreat.
I chose to move on,
as if newly born.
Renamed unrequited love- an infatuation.
Still numbness failed to yield sensation.
The chambers are busy,
kissing life with breath.
There is absolutely no room
for love or wrath.
Don't squeeze in through my love.
Don't ever squeeze in through.

The Swing

Begrimed tiny feet unconsciously drifted,

a ocean of longingness ebbing with tears.

Hearts collided and it rained.

A silent spectacle of unspoken words.

Infinite waves had hit the rock,

only a single tear drop melted it.

Pages of twin-subaqueous books

only he read, through its looks.

Now pointed to the girl next door's swing.

The cascade of golden shower unfolds a wing.

In the picturesque garden

works the father-craftsman

Sturdy and vibrant blooms her heart's desire.

Swinging her laughter and delight ever higher.

Wishes granted before you could wish,

Father's love is one such.

Memories are equatorial forests,

evergreen throughout and the farthest.

Time flies- strings of memories attached,

the tree, the swing, the craftsman, far detached.

She speaks her heart bold and clear,

Childhood memories of swing under the chandelier.

She adjured to the man she loved.

"conditions apply", he brutally abjured.

The shores of loving and being loved,

suddenly felt distantly apart.

Rivers of memories flow in between.

It Seems

Seems to be blessed,

seems to be a blessing,

seems to be a heavenly blessing of numerous gods,

seems to be guarded by a million guards,

seems to be wrapped in thousand flowers,

seems as if thrust between the clouds,

seems to be carried by oceans of joy,

seems to have sunk in caring warmth,

This is how I feel in your arms.

Safer, even in the greatest storms.

Can I stay here all my life?

Seem to have all I want.

Strong and Gentle

The imagination blend of unexpressed words,

Most awaited blossom of fresh flowers.

True fantasies of a longing heart,

Powerful bonds of inseparable past,

The meaning of every meaningless thoughts,

The germination of buried memories

The frequent peep of your dreams,

The tender look of your poetic eyes,

The manly ambitions of your winning mind.

Your energy, your spirit, your gentle force,

you may wear a thorn but you are a splendid rose.

Sand in an Hour Glass

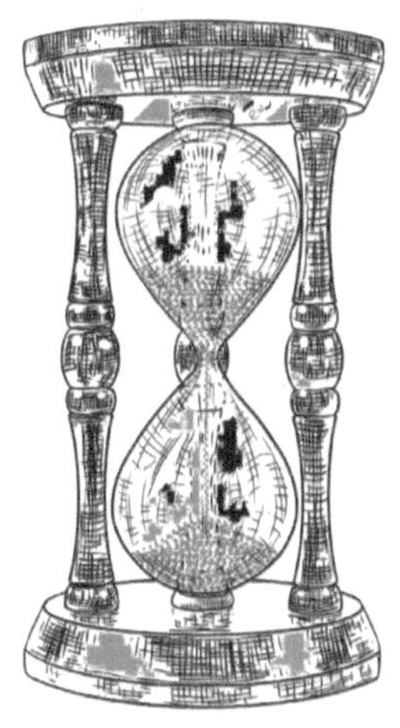

Like sand in an hour glass,

I pass through narrow passage of time.

Flipped up and down,

Oh! How I long for freedom.

I wish to be back in my hometown,

gazing stars on a moonlit night.

Shaped by loving hands,

kissed by the foamy waves,

sun-baked at the sweetest bays,

tickled by crazy crabs,

decked by seashells.

Here I stand guarding frontiers,

dreams dearer to heart slowly disappears.

Now I am back,

with breathless honour and soulful tears.

Still sealed in an hour glass,

Life has run out of time.

Please, "Let me hold my son"

The walls of the coffin intervene.

You,

'The Old Light House'

Dark and still stand out there,

mariners reach out to you no more.

Nothing is still the same,

but you still have 'light' in your name.

Never enroute your emotions, towards souls, that weigh not its worth.

When smiles squeeze through mountains of troubles-optimism

When frowns creep through tones of joy-pessimism

War and peace are Gemini twins,

What you choose to see, ultimately wins.

My actions, thoughts, future, present, dreams speak one word-YOU

My heart flutters with the pages when I write about you.

Strong citadels of faith turns to dust in no time,

raising a storm in a vacuum,

that neither past, present nor future can overcome.

May my hope and yours meet at the horizon of no hopes.

Crazier are the vibes of love's rhythm

I torment myself to love you less, still end up in loving you more, nevertheless.

I intend to take you to the best places. Bound by fate all I leave is traces.

Every heart has a tale to tell, to tell or not to tell, that's the difference.

You left,

Still you have left,

You have still left,

What is left is still left.

Life Shivers

Love Monopoly-betrayal destiny,

Infusing a progressive numbness.

The trees that outdid, met the axe.

What if my love outdid?

Strangely I realised all a stone,

I chiseled and chiseled,

Until it outshone.

The winter's charm of freezing layers,

Pleading warmth of melting favours.

More of takers, less of givers,

Life shivers.

CRAZY VIBES

Crazier vibes of the crazy heart,

My disposition dispart.

Travelling through the labyrinth of love,

The destination's destiny.

The more I repel

The more I travel

Mysteries constantly unravel

When, where and how,

The sparks lit and glow,

I ponder all the way

Why am I in love anyway?

QUEST

In quest

Of an intellectual companion,

To clink and sip

The poetical champagne,

Travelled through the reamy realms.

To where my lyrical heart dwells.

Yellowed with age,

Silvered with time,

Sweetened with rhyme.

Follow:

- @narmadhasatheeshkumar

- Narmadha Satheesh Kumar

www.ingramcontent.com/pod-product-compliance
Lightning Source LLC
La Vergne TN
LVHW041132150826
845673LV00007B/2287